A Travellers Guide to
Moder

By AUK Publications

1st edition

Copyright © 2021

All rights reserved.

Asatru UK Publications

Contents

Acknowledgements 4

About This Guide 5

Introduction to Heathenry 7

Heathenry in the Past 12

Who Are Asatru UK? 24

Gods 26

Spirits/Wights 34

Ancestors 40

Rituals 44

Runes, Seiðr and Galdr 65

Kindreds/Group Practice 73

Depression in a Heathen Context 81

Some Important Heathen Dates 89

Recommended Reading List 91

For my son Oscar and the next generation of Heathens

Acknowledgements

With thanks to H.J. Cronin, Gail, Jules, Rich and the rest of the Kin for putting this book together.

Thanks to Dean Kirkland for writing the segment titled 'blots' in the 'Rituals' chapter.

Thanks to Jules Mackinnon for her chapter on Runes, Seiðr and Galdr

Many thanks to Ross Downing for writing 'Bronze Age Heathenry' check out his links below...

https://www.ross-downing.com/

https://uhi.academia.edu/RossAlexanderDowning

About This Guide

This book is for all modern Heathens and those interested in the path. 'A Guide For Modern Heathenry' is not by any means a book where Asatru UK is dictating to you how you must practice. It is simply a guide for those who often ask us 'Where do I start?' or 'How do I do this?' While there will be some minor historical references, this is not a historical book, it is, as the title suggests about how some modern Heathens in the UK practice Heathenry.

It will be a very laid back account on Heathenry and any of the subjects listed can be researched in more depth using the books listed in our reading list.

Asatru UK has the largest presence of UK Heathens on social media. We meet four times a year for moots and have a very active Facebook page. Using experiences from some of our members and the members of the Kin, we have compiled some of the key elements of Heathenry including gods, ritual and group gatherings.

After each chapter, you will be a 'notes page' to write down anything you may wish to add or for quick reference.

Introduction to Heathenry

We can start by asking ourselves, what is Heathenry?

Heathenry in the modern form of the word, is the reconstruction of the ancient Northern European religion that has been lost for centuries. Before, during and for a small time after the 'Viking period', the peoples of Northern Europe did not have a name for their religion, it was simply a Worldview. What we mean by Worldview is that it is how they viewed the world, they grew up with it and it was just there. The gods can impact individual lives, as can the spirits but you are not obliged by scripture to worship them, nor are there any books with rules you must follow or a clergy telling you what to do.

Heathenry is a Polytheistic religion. This means we believe in multiple deities such as Odin, Thor and Freya. There are many other gods that form the Heathen pantheon and each god can have various names. For example, Odin has dozens, if not hundreds of names, such as Wotan, Woden, Alfather, Grimnir; just to name a few. For simplicity, we will use the common and familiar names for each of these gods.

Whilst a lot of people find comfort and fulfilment in group worship, Heathenry can be an individual path as well. What one Heathen believes may differ entirely from what another. Our own UPG or Unverified Personal Gnosis can form the basis of our faith. UPG is the direct experience a person may have with the gods in our religion. It is something that cannot be proven or even made sense of sometimes but it is a part of our faith. It's a very personal to us and can vary hugely from person to person.

Whilst people who worshiped the gods originate in Northern Europe, anybody can be Heathen. Don't think for a second because your ancestry originates from a different part of the world that you can't be Heathen. The gods are there whether we want to worship them or not. Sometimes they listen to our prayers and sometimes they do not.

There are many books you can look into for an in-depth look at what Heathenry is from either an academic or religious point of view. Much of what we do know today comes from historical sources such as the

Poetic Eddas along with archaeology. Heathenry is sometimes known as "the religion with homework" because of the amount of literature available to us. These books can often help make sense of our UPG in addition to giving us knowledge about how the ancient heathens used to practice.

Heathenry is a growing religion in the UK with many new people coming to the faith. Many people make the jump from pagan paths such as Wicca and Druidry to Heathenry because it speaks to them and fulfils them. One thing we will say that is important when you are new to Heathenry is to be careful where you source your reading materials (We will have a list at the back of this book). There are some dubious and outright racist people out there who often twist the religion to fit their own agenda.

Gods are not the only deities within Heathenry. The world is alive with creatures our eyes can see however, there are those we cannot, they are known as the hidden folk, wights or spirits. Whether you see them out the corner of your eye or have very personal experiences with them, the spirits of water, land and home are as much a part of Heathenry as the gods. Within Heathenry these spirits are often referred to as wights. Arguably the 'worship' of spirits is more important, according to some historical sources that is. We can talk more about the wights later.

There are rituals which can be done on your own, with your family, with a kindred or even a huge host of heathens gathered at a festival. Rituals can be very personal so we will later delve into an outline on how we perform rituals such as sumbels and blōts.

Seeking knowledge is important and is encouraged in Heathenry. Odin even teaches us this. Never be afraid to ask questions from experienced Heathens or even attend one of your local kindred moots (More on kindreds later). Welcome to Heathenry, Asatru UK hopes you find this book useful!

Notes

Heathenry in the Past

Bronze Age Heathenry

Compared to "Norse Heathendom", or the Viking era and the sources we associate with that period, the Bronze Age is considerably longer. The insights into the Viking period material spans from the Vendel period to the mid-medieval period, about 500 years at the most generous estimation, with most of that being the written sources some 200 or more years after the period they describe.

In contrast, the Nordic Bronze Age has no written sources, but there is substantial archaeology and the majority of which definitely has clear religious character. The Nordic Bronze Age spans the years 1700-500 BC, i.e. beginning nearly 4000 years ago. One problem with this dating is that the "end" does not satisfactorily explain the cultural changes that bleed into the pre-Roman Iron Age and (pre-Vendel) Migration Era 500BC-375CE. Suffice it to say that the Nordic Bronze Age begins roughly at the end of the Mesopotamian

Bronze Age, the period in the Mediterranean which saw the birth of the Babylonian Empire, start of the Egyptian New Kingdom, and perhaps most influentially; the rise of the Mycenaean civilisation. The end of the Nordic Bronze Age corresponds roughly to the Greco-Persian Wars. Therefore, one is inclined to see the Nordic Bronze Age as somehow linked to Greek civilisation. Swedish rock carvings have been theorised as echoing Homeric Age ideas, and Nordic Bronze Age art such as "horned Helmets" (again a symbolism even found later in Vendel period Scandinavia and Germanic Britain) are probably directly influenced by Greek culture.

It is important to see the Nordic Bronze Age in terms of the wider European social context. The reason being is that we see considerable trade over vast distances, it is assumed that such connections were leapfrogging rather than actual Greeks sailing straight to Sweden.

However, there is evidence of individuals travelling vast distances in their lifetime, and these are often in ritual contexts. For example, the Egtved girl burial in Denmark (c. 1390–1370 BC) was from the German border with Switzerland. A number of metalworking artefacts show specific trade deep into the European continent. This, coupled with the transport of bronze objects and the similarity with designs over large areas, gives the impression that Nordic Bronze Age religion was likely heavily influenced by southern ideas. If we look at what was happening in the Mediterranean parallel to what was happening in the north, we can only wonder about the tales and religious ideas that were forming.

For the interests of Heathens, there are some fascinating hints at gods which would later appear in Viking Age material. However, scholars are reticent to participate in such speculation.

Rock carvings of divine feet hint at Njord, figures with hammers and goat drawn chariots hint at Thor, twin gods call to mind Balder and Hother, or the type of divine ancestors such as Hengest and Horsa. Castor and Pollux, Romulus and Remus, would be southern parallels.

This era produces a considerable amount of boat imagery, and many ritual sites and burials are found in close proximity to water. This should not be considered entirely symbolic, however, since if most people lived and travelled along waterways it would in fact by especially significant if a burial or ritual site was placed a large distance inland away from areas of habitation. However, most scholars agree that ritual and burial sites near water was a significant symbolic relationship.

For Heathens, the most obvious suspicion is that this is the start of the Frey and Freya ship mythology, and perhaps even the formation of Scandinavian maritime culture that would eventually lead to the Viking dominance, some 1500 years later.

As with the other periods, there seems some awareness of the past, with sites such as impressive burial structure at Kivik being built on a Stone Age settlement, and possible deposits of Stone Age tools replaced in the newly built Bronze Age structure. Similarly, rock carving sites have in some cases seen large stones placed on the stone plateau as with cracks in the rock face and in some cases hundreds of flint tools such as arrowheads placed in the gap.

Rock carvings during this period also show consistent relationship with water, fresh water often stream over these carved rock faces perhaps directly into the sea or river where the petroglyphs were made.

Petroglyphs themselves have been the subject of considerable study and cross-referenced with local Bronze Age archaeology and artefacts. Current scholarship on Nordic petroglyphs has been something of an inversion of other academic disciplines, whilst most scholars have moved away from comparative studies of societies separated by time and space, petroglyphs studies have moved from the tunnel-vision of local amateur antiquaries to being placed in the context of other world heritage sites. The academic reasoning behind this is that petroglyphs are extremely specific a subject, and perhaps show commonalities in psychology and physical process, all over the world. Therefore, new theories and insights into Scandinavian rock carvings have emerged from scholars studying African or American rock carvings, with especial focus on bringing to light ancient religious cosmology.

One remarkable feature of the Nordic Bronze Age is that metal artefacts show a consistently high level of expertise, the artistic detail, metallurgical knowledge, and sheer craftsmanship largely outshine that found anywhere else in the world at this time. Scholars have placed significant focus on the probability of smiths having religious office and strong social status, in this period. Since Iron Age stories consistently talk of divine smiths, and magical metal artefacts, it seems reasonable to assume that these ideas began in the Bronze Age.

The introduction of farming was a significant cultural development, and must have been consciously considered so for a long time during this period. The majority of rock carvings show ploughing, and the religious importance of the plough itself. Chariots and the introduction of the wheel are also primary concerns for the rock carvers. Heathens may consider Tacitus' reference to a holy wagon of Nerthus, to the Viking Age references to Frey's wagon, to Freya's cat-drawn chariot, and to Gefjun's ploughing. The rock carvings are so diverse, enigmatic, and often bizarre that a personal investigation of the images cannot be recommended enough.

Viking Age Heathenry

The Viking Age is the name scholars often give to the period spanning the years 793-1066. The Vikings are often imagined to be Scandinavians, but the Viking Age starts with a Scandinavian attack on England, and ends with one of many invasions of Scandinavians into England. Most of the people we call Vikings didn't live in Scandinavia, by definition they were raiders, traders and settlers so they existed mainly outside of Scandinavia and in many cases were living for generations or even centuries outside of Scandinavia. For example, Russia, Ireland and Norman France all had Viking populations for over 150 years. Wherever people go they interact with the people already in those places, and this is what happened with Viking Heathens.

Our two main sources for Heathendom in the Viking Age are from written sources and from archaeological remains. Most of the records we have for the mythology of the Vikings were written hundreds of years after the Vikings. These records were mainly made in Iceland, Denmark and the British Isles and were documenting an oral tradition. Viking Heathens used an oral culture of live poetry performance to remember their myths, those songs that survived the conversion to Christianity were eventually written down by people like Snorri Sturluson, and Saxo Grammaticus, who wanted to preserve the history and culture of northern European heritage.

Runes were also an important part of Viking cultures but most people could not read and write in runes and they were probably only used by specialists. In some cases, runes survived long after the Vikings and were used as a common form of writing or as a magical alphabet. Runestones are what most people associate with runes, but these were only one aspect of runes in the Viking Age. Runestones mainly exist in Sweden and are tombstone-type memorials, most of them are Christian or a mix of Christian and Heathen. This religious mix is called 'syncretic', which means hybrid or 'two religions at the same time'. The Viking Age can be defined as the historical period of syncretic religions, where Heathendom was ending- not flourishing.

We have many examples of Viking Heathendom that shows Christian influence, but this does not mean that it was less Heathen- only that Heathens were adapting as they always had. Most people couldn't imagine that Christianity would one day be the only official and legal religion in all of Europe and Russia. Scholars look at Viking Heathendom as people living their lives and expressing themselves with the gods, rituals, myths and acceptable practices of the people around them at each time and place. Therefore, we cannot say that how Vikings were worshipping Thor in England in the year 1050 was the same way of being Heathen when Vikings were burying their dead in Russia in 925 some 3000 km away.

It is important to not fall into the trap of wishful thinking about the Vikings, nor to take for granted that what most people think about Viking Heathendom is true. Christians in England made laws against Anglo-Saxons and Vikings practicing Heathenship (living the religion of Heathendom). In conclusion, the following points are also supported from later saga sources and archaeology:

- Foretelling the future and consulting witches
- Asking witches to make spells for love and to cause people's deaths

- Worshipping trees
- Worshipping wells
- Worshipping stones
- Worshipping and meditating at spots of natural beauty
- Worshipping gods in the form of animals
- Worshipping idols
- Offering parts of animals used for food (animal sacrifice) to idols
- Offering valuable objects (gold, jewellery) at wells, swamps and to idols
- Burying the dead with valuable objects to take to the afterlife
- Burying sacrificed animals and humans with the dead to go with them in the afterlife
- Naming children by touching them with soil

We also have evidence from other sources for:
- Naming children with water
- Eating and drinking in common meals at rituals
- Rituals accompanied by poetry, music and acting out myths

- Some actors wearing masks, hoods and cloaks at rituals
- Rituals mainly taking place in a hall or by outdoor fires lit at an ancient site
- Pillars inside the hall the main focus of ritual
- Poles at ancient sites the main focus of ritual

Notes

Who Are Asatru UK?

Asatru UK or AUK for short started as a Facebook group in 2012 to bring UK Heathens together. By 2013 and after a reform the group had 600 members and the Kin were formed. As of writing this in 2020 the group now has almost 3000 members with dozens joining each week.

The Kin are the administrators who run the group and organise real world events, which is always the goal of AUK; to bring Heathens together in real life. Asatru UK runs on a principle of being an inclusive Heathen group. We take the process of vetting new members to the Facebook group very seriously, so that we can keep the group welcoming and to abide by our inclusive founding principles.

The first moot (gathering) was in the beginning of 2013 in York, a city which has hosted AUK on an annual basis ever since; in addition AUK also hosts a summer camp and an autumn moot. The Asgardian Heathen

Festival also originated from AUK and saw hundreds of UK heathens meet to socialise and celebrate the faith.

Asatru UK prides itself on its inclusive identity and is often praised by its members for being a safe and welcoming place. On a lighter note, AUK is commended for not being a group full of repetitive memes and political debates. This inclusive and constructive approach on AUK has inspired a number of smaller regional groups, bringing Heathens together, which in turn led to the Confederation of UK Heathen Kindreds.

We have also branched out into selling branded merchandise as well as publishing books, including our very popular "Travel Hávámal". We are currently expanding our work by working towards gaining charity status, commissioning godposts for a portable Vé (sacred space), and raising funds for our long-term aim to purchase land to build a temple. We work closely with groups who share our values across Britain and internationally, with AUK representatives regularly attending international moots and conferences.

Gods

There is a case for the gods being the main reason people are first drawn to Heathenry. Many Heathens that join Asatru UK come to the religion after an experience with an individual or multiple gods, be it in dreams, visions or physical experiences. There is also the draw from the age-old stories of the gods, not everybody has an experience. These aren't just gods that preach peace, conversion and happiness, these are also gods of war, fertility, wrath and sometimes cunning.

What is the exact nature of our gods? To put it simply we just don't know. It is safe to say that the gods are far beyond our understanding and knowledge. We are mortals here on Midgard who have limited knowledge of the world and universe around us. We have stories about the gods and their names can be found throughout history. We do believe however that the 'old' gods are real and never really went away when the Christian god came. They were only forgotten.

Even the names of the gods can be contested depending on the heathenry you follow. There are many types of heathen paths from Anglo-Saxon to Frankish to the more common Norse. As mentioned before we will use the Norse names for any gods we mention as there tends to be more heathens who follow the Norse path.

Some people experience close bonds with gods whilst others keep their distance. Everybody has a different experience when it comes to gods. It is quite widely accepted however that when you ask a god for something, be very wary about what you ask them for because a god might just give you what you want however it may not be the outcome you expect and may not always be good.

More times often than not a god may come to you or take notice of you. How or why may not be answered for a while if at all. Some people have what's known as a 'patron god', a single god that they worship above the others. This is not a necessity or even that common as we follow a polytheistic religion.

The key to connecting to a god, if this is what you really want, is to honour them regularly through offerings and ritual. They may not always be listening as they are not omnipresent however one day they might. Your intent in Heathenry is just as important as the deed itself.

Don't be disheartened or upset if you can't connect with a god, one day you might but it is not an important part of Heathenry. Ancient Heathens often honoured and worshiped the spirits of the house, farm and land more so than the gods themselves. We will speak more about spirits and wights in another chapter.

So to summarise, the gods are important but are not necessarily a vital part of your heathenry. Do what feels right to you and maybe a god will take notice.

Which gods?

Being a polytheist religion, we have a multitude of gods and goddesses to choose from. The principal pantheon in Heathenry are those made up of the Æsir (Aesir) and Vanir. The Æsir are gods such as Odin, Thor and Tyr whilst the Vanir comprise of Njord, Freyja and Freyr amongst others. The two were separate tribes before a war amongst them brought them together under one pantheon. More information on this war can be found in the Edda's.

A very common thought process for many new Heathens is how does one connect to Odin or Thor or Freya. These three are among a number of gods we are most familiar with and are likely the first gods you will encounter on any Google search.

However! There are so many gods and paths you can learn about so don't be immediately drawn to the Alfather, unless that is what feels right for you of course. Some people worship just the Vanir or just the Aesir. Some people worship the gods and spirits of the sea whilst others worship the Jotuns as gods. There are even some people who worship the 'darker' deities such as Hel. As you can see, Heathenry is a very broad religion with many paths you can take and mingle together.

Some Heathens also share their gods with other pantheons such as the Celtic pantheons or the Roman ones. It is known that as people conquered or migrated throughout history they brought their gods with them so the idea of mixing pantheons isn't a new thing.

Offerings

A common question is often what shall I offer to this god or that god? Have a look at the stories and literature featuring that god to see what they are inclined to accept. Also ask your peers for their experiences when offering to gods. For Odin as an example, an offering of wine. A good starting point for most gods however is generally alcohol, seasonal fruit or meat. Rituals and offerings will be discussed in more depth in a later chapter.

It is accepted among Heathens that blood sacrifice is not a necessity in the modern world. Our ancestors lived during extremely tough times where they worked from sunrise to sunset, ate little and knew little of the world outside of their home. Animal sacrifice may have been the drastic thing they needed to do to ask for help from the gods.

The Gods and Goddesses

We are using the list of Aesir gods as described by Snorri Sturluson in Skaldskaparmal (the Prose Edda) however, it's worth noting that Snorri is very inconsistent. For example, he lists Thor's daughter as a goddess but not his sons as gods. In Gylfaginning he states Eir is a goddess, but in Skaldskaparmal, she is listed a Valkyrie. A number of scholars have questioned if Snorri made up some of the goddesses because they appear nowhere else in any skaldic poetry and only in Skaldskaparmal. Where a goddess is in dispute we have left her out, on the basis that there are plenty without them. In addition, we have added a few in on the basis that as modern heathens we include them as gods.

Gods:

Odin - the Allfather, Chief of the Gods of Asgard and God of wisdom.

Thor - God of Thunder, Protector of Asgard and Midgard

Yngvi-Freyr (or just Freyr) - Vanir hostage and God of Fertility

Vidar - Odin's Avenger who kills Fenrir and survives Ragnarok

Baldr - known as the Bright God, is killed by his brother who was tricked by Loki. Baldr will return from Hel after Ragnarok.

Vali - Baldr's Avenger who also survives Ragnarok

Heimdall - Guardian of the Gods and Father of Mankind

Tyr - God of Sky and War, lost his hand during the binding of Fenrir

Njord - Vanir Hostage, God of Fertility, Wealth and Wind.

Bragi - God of Poetry and Wisdom

Hod - blind son of Odin tricked into killing his brother Baldr by Loki. Joins his brother Baldr on his return from Hel after Ragnarok

Forseti - God of Justice

Loki - seen as a God of Mischief but is a pivotal figure in the stories of the gods.

Hoenir - Aesir hostage following the Aesir\Vanir War, Aesir told the Vanir he was the wisest among them

Mimir - Aesir hostage and wise God whose head the Vanir sent back to Odin when they realised that Hoenir was not as wise as the Aesir said. Odin magically preserved Mimirs head.

Goddesses:

Frigg - wife of Odin, and his adversary in their games with human lives

Freya - Vanir, Goddess of Fertility, Magic and Love

Fulla - Friggs secret keeper

Gerd - Jotun wife of Freyr, seen as an Earth Goddess

Gefion - turned her 4 sons into bulls and ploughs Zealand away from Scandinavia

Gna - Frigg's messenger

Skadi - Jotun wife of Njord and later Odin, seen as a Goddess of Winter

Idunn - Keeper of the Apples of Youth who is married to Bragi

Nanna - wife of Baldr and mother of Forseti

Hnoss - daughter of Freya and Odr

Rind - mother of Vali

Siofn - Goddess of Marriage\Relationships

Saga - Odin's drinking partner

Sigyn - Loki's wife

Sif - Wife of Thor with magical golden hair, often associated with summer and harvests

Var - Goddess of Marriage\Relationships

Thrud - Thor's daughter

Ran - Goddess in who's hall those who drown at sea reside

Eir - missed off the list in Skaldskaparmal but attested in Gylfaginning, Eir is seen as the Goddess of Healing.

Notes

Spirits/Wights

The worship or honouring of spirits is a very important part of Heathenry. Now, when we say spirits we don't necessarily mean ghosts that haunt a particular location. The spirits are the beings that inhabit a location as a human does, they are also known as the hidden folk for they are mostly invisible to the naked eye. There are many types of spirits from domestic ones to land spirits, water spirits to ones that dwell on farms. They are everywhere and should be respected.

Historically these spirits and others such as Dwarves or Elves, Nisse etc were often worshipped as demigods and played a larger part in individual people's lives then the gods themselves. This is simply because the deity has a much more vested interest in what you do day to day as they are living with you. The ancient people included them in almost all aspects of their lives from where they construct a home to even the minute details like the first time they step over the threshold. Even in the modern day, there are stories in Iceland where plans for the construction of a road have to be altered to avoid a place where spirits dwell, for example a road.

The ancestors believed the spirits inhabited every part of nature some believed that raw materials used to build a house would also bring the spirits with said raw materials. Others believed that where a dwelling was built the spirits of that land would then inhabit the house thus becoming a domestic spirit.

How Do I Build a Relationship With a Spirit?

If you have one of the hidden folk dwelling in your property or your land then it is important for you to build a relationship with it. Most of the time you won't notice their presence but this doesn't mean they aren't there. Spirits that are ignored may cause a little bit of mischief or just simply move on to another location. It's amazing what positive energy you can build from frequent offerings and some respect.

Start with your altar in the corner of the room. The energy from a spirit is often drawn to the corners of rooms. With all respect think of it as dust that is pushed to the corner effortlessly, it is the same with the energy of a spirit.

You can even name the spirit or ask it for its name, pay attention to any signs or dreams you may have where you find the spirits name. Treat it like a lodger in your home, speak to it and offer food. It's a two way thing rather than just what you'd like to gain.

Think if it like building a relationship with a person, you start off with small, polite gestures without demanding anything until you build a rapport and are in a place where you can request things from the spirit. But remember there is the gift cycle in Heathenry where if you ask for something, always give something in return.

Example of offerings can be grain, oats, milk, seasonal fruit and any other perishable item. Find out what works and then use that. Leave it over night or for the day and then you can dispose of it.

As with gods, don't be disheartened if you can't build a relationship with your spirit or even if you don't have a spirit. Some spirits may have left decades before you moved in, throughout history families often dwelt in the same location for generations and the wights were attached to the family as well as the home. In the modern world we move around so much that we need to adapt to this. Keep making your offerings and eventually something might just come along. Always be careful what you invite into your home though.

If you or a kindred you belong to want to build a relationship with the spirits in the wild then follow the same structure as a domestic spirit. Offerings and respecting the land i.e. tidying up rubbish left by people, keeping the area nice and always offer bio gradable offerings. Also, be wary of bringing Iron into a sacred space as this was always believed to fend off spirits.

The honouring or worship of spirits can sometimes be a very spiritually fulfilling part of Heathenry. Consistency is key, keep it up and you may be rewarded.

Notes

Ancestors

It is generally accepted amongst heathens that in modern day heathenry there is a taste for ancestor veneration or at least honouring your ancestors. Cultures all over the world venerate their ancestors through ritual, stories and deeds. There is no reason why heathens wouldn't do this too.

We don't tend to worship ancestors only honouring them and remembering them. How can we do this? It can be pretty fun and a huge history lesson. If you want to know more look into your family history be it using online sources or speaking to your living relatives. This will in turn create an image of individuals in your family tree and give names to your ancestors.

Honouring Ancestors

There are many different ways we can honour our ancestors once we discover who they are. Please note though; if you are in a position where you are unaware of whom your ancestors are or you do not have the means to find out, you can toast to ancestors known and unknown.

One way we can honour our ancestors is to include them in our home rituals, if you have pictures then great if not, it's not necessary. Toast them with a drink, call out their names and hail them. Some people even set out an ancestor's plate at the dinner table. Light a candle and offer a few words to them.

We can also honour them in a Sumbel, calling out their names as you raise a horn or a glass, praising the deeds they have done or what they may have taught you.

A third way you can honour your ancestors is by simply talking about them to others. Passing on war stories from a grandparent, advice from a mother or father, a family joke or struggle. Keep them alive through these stories and remember the good times with those you were lucky to know.

It should be noted too that if the ancestors you know of were unpleasant characters then you could choose not to honour them. You can always choose to honour someone you respect or has made a difference in your life. You can even miss this aspect of heathenry out completely if it doesn't fit into your worldview.

That is one of the reasons it is so important to make a good name for yourself in life so you are remembered that way after death.

Your ancestors will live on for as long as you remember them, this is how we are remembered when we pass on from this world.

Notes

Rituals

What is a ritual and why do we do it? A ritual is a way of us connecting to the deities of our religion by giving thanks, asking for advice/aid or seeking a deeper connection. It can also be to the spirits or our ancestors. Whilst ancestor reverence may not have been centre to the ancient heathens, many modern heathens do practice this to build a closer relationship to those that have passed on. There are a few types of ritual that you can perform, the two main ones are Blots and Sumbels. The former being more ceremonial and the latter being informal.

There are some great books on rituals, our ancestors worshipped and honoured the spirits of the farm or land more so than the gods in some cases. Building a relationship with your house wight or land wight is an important part of some heathens practices, that's if you have a house wight, not everybody does.

Home Rituals

A number of Heathens do rituals at home on their own or with family members. These are performed to create a closer relationship to your house spirit, honour a god or contact your ancestors.

So what can you do at home? It could be beneficial to have an altar where the energy of the deity can manifest and centre around. Historical sources and modern accounts tend to lean to the corner of a room being the centre of a manifestation.

If you want to offer to a house spirit, say some words aloud as if the spirit is a person standing beside you. Let them hear your words clearly. Leave an offering; it can be anything however, oats or milk are a popular choice. Regular offerings can help towards building that relationship. Use this same method in your garden or a local woodland/stream/sacred space. Even in busy metropolitan areas there will be spirits there that you can build connections with. Do not forget about the hidden folk!

Some Heathens like to have regular rituals to gods at home, whether it's to one deity or multiple ones.

Wherever your sacred spot is at home, be it an altar or not, you can perform the ritual here. Some only perform rituals during the solstices or important times of year. Others, not at all. Whilst it is not mandatory to being heathen, regular rituals are a great way to be better connected spiritually to the religion.

Think of the god you are offering to, from your own experience as well as anything you may have read from historical sources to decide what to offer. For example, Thors journey to Utgarda-loki he challenges the giant to a drinking contest, so some ale or beer would suffice as an offering. For Odin, wine. For Freyr or Freya, grain and eggs. These are merely examples, do what feels right to you.

Say some words to the gods but always be warned, the gods are powerful beings far beyond our understanding. If you swear an oath then be prepared to keep that oath. Any words you share with the gods need to be well thought of. If a god answers then it is likely they will need you more then you need them or the outcome may be what you asked for but the journey there may not be pleasant. Sometimes it is safe just keeping a blōt to a god as thanks.

Ancestors ... to connect ... relatives the ... speak to the ... when I talk t...

Whilst an ... obvious forn... clear signs. ... get what you ...

listen to what you have to say, and consi...
you make to them. However, for nev...
to consider what the wights hav...
the life they have already gi...
food on your table, guide...
always best to start ...
already have. Do...
gratitude and ...
return an...
wights
fo...

A blōt (pronounced 'bloat') is part of the gifting cycle, and the gifting cycle was essential in heathen society. I'm often asked by people new to heathenry who should I pray to for healing, or to achieve x, and the answer is to whichever god you already have a relationship with, because if you don't already have a relationship with them it's like asking a stranger in the street for help. Blōt is the way we begin to build that relationship with the gods and wights, and get their attention.

In technical terms blōt builds mægan or honour, the more mægan you have the more likely the wights are to

r any requests
'eathens you have
already done for you,
ven you, your family, the
ice from the ancestors, so it's
st by saying thanks for what you
blōt a couple of times just in general
without asking for anything specifically in
you will begin to gain the respect of the
, your mægan goes up, then you can start to ask
other things in blōt or in prayer.

So who can we blōt to? You can perform a blōt to honour any wight (spirit), and it's only limited by your imagination. You can blōt to the gods, the ancestors, the giants or Jötunns (often important in healing if part of your belief is that they're responsible for the illness), the Alvar (elves) and Duergar (dwarves), your house wights, the land wights and plant wights in the local area etc. It is however best just to stick to wights from the Germanic or mythology, for a very simple reason. A Celtic deity, for example, is used to receiving offerings in a very specific way usually in a more druidic type ritual, so in order to show respect to these other gods it's probably best to stick to the form of ritual they expect.

From the lore we can see that a basic formal blōt had 6 separate parts;

1) Create Sacred space
2) Set the intention (purpose)
3) Invite in the wights
4) Bless the offering
5) Make the offering
6) Close

Beyond this, a blōt is pretty free form and it is generally down to the individual goði (ritual leader) to come up with their own words. Historically a lot of this would probably be done in Skaldic verse, though this is not so important these days, and many people manage by taking appropriate passages from the lore.

For example in creating sacred space; heathens do not work with classic elements or four directions and therefore do not cast a circle. In fact, from what we know about sacred space it was usually square or rectangular.

Probably the most traditional way of creating sacred space is to carry live fire around the perimeter or if there are a number of people involved all walking round the perimeter chanting something appropriate can also be used.

Setting the intention, as in all rituals, is arguably the most important part of the ritual. Energy flows where thought goes, so it's vital to have a clear purpose to the ritual, and to explain that purpose to anybody who's attending so they know what's expected and when so can add their energy to yours. This doesn't have to be complicated in fact in most cases the simpler the better. Example: 'We are gathered here today to perform a blōt to Odin to ask for your protection this Winter's night' etc.

The invitation is usually done in a specific way and follows the format of heathen prayer, usually by first reciting the lineage if it's known, 'Hail Odin Borsson, Husband of Frigg, father of Thor', etc. Then reciting some of their major deeds that relate to the purpose of the ritual. For example: 'You hung on the word tree for nine days and nights without food or drink to enable the runes to enter the nine realms and enable us to use them for our protection' etc. Then what you want the deity to do 'please join our ritual/ve this night'.

Blessing the offering: example, 'Odin bless this offering fill it with your wisdom and might- hail Odin'. It's usual at this stage of the ritual to take a bit of the offering itself and give a bit to the people who are attending to sip or nibble, sometimes they can also be sprinkled with the offering all of this means that they the blessing of the wights/ gods inside themselves. Just a little bit of good luck to help with whatever their facing in their lives at that moment.

Make the offering. There are a range of ways this can be done, the ritual leader can just make the offering by putting it into a bowl. It can also be split between everyone attending so they can make a personal offering to their own deity. At the end of the ritual, all offerings should be put onto the ground.

Closing! At this stage it is important to thank all the gods and wights that took part. It is also customary to thank the other people who took part. . The sacred space and the footprint of the energy of the ritual will naturally slowly fade, but as they do so they'll help to increase the energy of the land it was held on and of the local land wights. The more you repeat ritual in the same place the more energy you will add. However, if it's likely that the site will be disturbed by anyone who is likely to interfere with or mess up the energy, then it's better to close sacred space by simply doing whatever you did to create it in reverse. Over time, you learn to trust your own intuition about whether sacred space needs closing or not.

Anybody can join in a blōt, they don't necessarily have to be heathen. But effectively in blōt you are trying to make a connection to the heathen gods and wights, to many people this would be classed as an occult practice or against their existing beliefs, and even though it's perfectly safe with people who've never been involved in anything like this before it can still be quite scary. They have to understand that there is a chance that the wights will respond and begin to take an interest in anybody who is present, because that's basically what we are doing it for. So people have to be comfortable with that to take part. If people are not comfortable participating they should always be welcome to watch, as long as they're quiet and respectful. All the energies of the ritual should be contained within the sacred space, it's one of the reasons we create it. So no one watching from outside of the sacred space should be affected by anything that happens inside it.

A lot of solitary heathens celebrate a blōt as a central part of their personal practices. So you don't necessarily need to be in a group. Without a large sacred space to create and maintain, other people to explain what's happening and tell them what to do and using very simple prayers and invocations an effective blōt doesn't need a lot of equipment and can be completed in about 10 minutes.

Sumbel/Symbel

Unlike a blot, the Sumbel is a more informal ritual to perform within a group. We say informal but it is just as important and if not more important than a blot. We can gather from historical sources such as Beowulf and the Scandinavian sagas that Sumbel were performed by the peoples of that time.

Sumbels can be performed with anything from a couple people to hundreds and theoretically thousands, even though we may reach Ragnarok before a thousand person Sumbel actually finishes! It can be done in your home where the host would usually lead or in your garden or in your local sacred place, basically anywhere. Any person, not necessarily a Gothi can lead a Sumbel.

So how to carry out a three round Sumbel. The host or the person leading will declare the Sumbel after the blot, at the end of the gathering or in the middle of the night around a fire. Three rounds will follow, first to the gods, second to the spirits of the land and thirdly to your ancestors.

Within your group, you usually form a circle. A horn or drinking vessel is filled with mead or an alcoholic beverage, a non-alcoholic beverage is also advisable for children or adults who don't drink.

The horn is passed around the circle clockwise. During the first round, you declare to a god/goddess or gods/ess of your choice. If you do not wish to bellow out the name of your chosen deity you can say it quietly or pass the horn to the next person. You never have to take part. After hailing the god, you take a sip of drink from the horn.

For example, I would shout, "Hail Freyr, lord of the harvest, lord of love and fertility. I honour you and your deeds. Hail Freyr!!". To which the other participants would echo the call of 'Hail Freyr'. (You can just say Hail [insert god/ess] rather than say a whole sentence) So on and so forth until the horn returns to the host.

Next, we have a round to the spirits of the land. We need to honour the spirits as it is their land as well as ours. We should remember them and not ignore them. Just like the god round you raise the horn, hail the spirits of the land or home and then take a sip of drink or even splash a bit on the ground as an offering to the land spirits.

Lastly, we have the round dedicated to the ancestors. Just like the previous two rounds the horn is passed around and the person with the horn can call out a declaration to their ancestors. You can just say, "Hail to my Ancestors" or go in-depth and name those who have passed on before you, remembering their names and their deeds. Not just family but close friends or kindred members who have passed too.

There are other versions of Sumbels that can be performed but this is the most common one and one we usually perform.

There is also fourth or bonus round to finish the mead if you do not wish to offer it. This round is toasts and boasts. You pass around the horn as you have done before and can call out a toast to a friend or family member if they have accomplished something recently or helped you in some way. You can also boast about something you achieved recently for example that new job, a new success, a new child etc. this is a free round where you can generally say whatever you want.

Remember as with all religious rites, it is important to respect other peoples turns with the horns by listening and taking in their personal stories or hails.

That concludes the Sumbel. Try it with friends, family or your kindred. It is a great way of bringing the community together whilst practicing Heathenry. After many Sumbels performed together, the group will have made memories, some you will look back on in the future and smile or laugh at.

Note on Creating Altars

Altars are very personal to Heathens so it is difficult to say exactly how to make one and what to fill it with. Therefore, we can only give suggestions. Have some sort of stand to balance the items i.e. a stall or a small table, anything really to start with. Generally, on an altar you will have a godpost or an image of a god or totem (These aren't necessary, you can call upon any god or spirit you choose). Next, we have an offering bowl where we can place the offerings we will be making to the deity and that is about it really. Some people choose to have an altar cloth and candles too.

Do not worry about rushing into getting stuff for the altar i.e. special items such as jewellery, things you find in nature or gifts etc. These accumulate over time and you can add to the altar as you go.

It is important to remember to respect the altar and keep it tidy as the more you use it the more energy will build around it. You will be using it to connect with deities after all.

Note on Oaths

Oaths are extremely personal and important promises and deals you make with a deity. Be advised, you are potentially entering an agreement that will be there for the rest of your life and an oath is sometimes big enough to gain the notice of a god. Take time and think about if it is something you really want and think of all the potential outcomes of said oath, it may not always turn out the way you want it to. It's unadvisable to make one when you are intoxicated or your mind is too occupied. Just be wary and don't take an oath lightly.

Whilst in a marriage you make promises to each other these are more often than not a legal contract rather than an actual oath. If you are in a bad place or things just aren't working then there is no obligation to stay as you will not be breaking an oath.

It's also worth noting that if you are tricked into taking an oath by somebody, then it has not come from your own heart or mind. That oath doesn't count. Always have a witness if you can so you can be supported and held to account.

Any oaths you make with other people you can ask to be released from them and if it is mutually agreed then said oath no longer stands.

Notes

Afterlife

A common question for new heathens is about the afterlife. This is usually because the society we live in is heavily influenced by the heaven and hell in Christianity. Soon in Heathenry, you generally realise that it's all about how you live your life and making the most of every moment, small and large.

When it comes to the afterlife in modern day Heathenry, concepts vary from Heathen to Heathen. We can give you a number of different ideas to give you something to think about. These are taken from some historical sources as well as a general UPG from UK Heathens.

Halls of the Gods. Now let's talk about the most known place, Valhalla. Valhalla is often mistaken for a sort of 'Heathen Heaven', which is not strictly true. Those who die in battle or combat are split between Freyjas hall Sessrúmnir, in Fólkvangr and Odin's hall Valhalla. Half-and-half, Freyja chooses the first half whilst Odin the second. This is all preparation for

Ragnarok where the chosen will fight. Unless you are a soldier or a warrior then Valhalla is not a place the average person would want to be. Endless fighting and death repeated over and over again, day after day. There is even a case for gaining entry to the halls of the other gods. One such is Ran's Hall, where those that die at sea will go.

Helheim. Helheim or Hel is one of the 9 worlds where the majority of the dead go; those that die of sickness or old age etc. The goddess Hel according to some sources possibly rules over Helheim. Hel is a dull land not much different from ours where you go to be at one with your ancestors in their halls, an afterlife not much different from your life on Midgard. There is potential and correlation for Hel to be another concept for the Burial Mound.

Another concept is Reincarnation. Not the sort where you are reborn in another body but reincarnation where you pass on your genes to your descendants. This is scientifically proven and visible to the naked eye. You may look like your parent or your grand parent or your great grandparent and so on. This concept enforces that how you live has an effect on those you leave behind. A family reputation can be easy to tarnish and hard to repair. It also shows how important it is to pass on as much knowledge to your children as possible.

The ultimate answer to the question though is we just don't know. There is no answer because we have no hard proof. The notion of an afterlife is mainly there to give comfort to the living that death is not necessarily the end. Do not live your life worrying or preparing for an afterlife we know little about, use your time to live your life and be the best you can be.

Notes

Runes, Seiðr and Galdr

There are many ways in which people of the past have worked with energy and divination, or magic. We have very little information about actual practices and techniques from late Iron Age Europe but there are many people who practice magic in different forms today. Some of the methods from the past that have survived in written text are: seiðr, Galdr and Runic magic.

Practitioners of seiðr (Say-ther) are said to have communed with gods and Spirits to tell people of the future and at times attempt to change the course of fate. They were seers, givers of prophecy, blessings and curses. They could expose the hidden information unseen by others. They travelled from town to town and were treated with great respect but also feared.

Galdr can be performed with runes and with words of a chant or song. These sounds can be repeated again and again with intent to raise large amounts of energy that can be directed into magical channels.

Runic magic. Runes can be used in many ways, for divination, curses and healing just to name a few. The most beneficial way to use runic energy is for self-reflection and improvement, to follow the path to wisdom as Odin does.

The best way to gain familiarity with your runes is to draw one every day. Draw a rune in the morning and keep its properties in mind during the day.

For example if you drew Tiwaz you would keep strength and courage in mind all day, remembering to face your fears and do what's needed. Or if you drew Nauthiz you would concentrate on only putting your energy towards the things that you actually need deep down, remembering to not get caught up in the trivialities of the day.

Elder Futhark

Below is a list of the Elder Futhark runes and their properties. There is also a guide as to how to pronounce this although that will depend on entirely where you are.

Fehu
"Fay-who" ᚠ

Cattle
Wealth is the source of discord amongst kin. The wolf lives in the forest.
Mobile property
Wealth put to use
New beginings
Possessions won or earned
A sign of hope and plenty
Closely connected to Hamingja (luck)
Helps to facilitate the exchange of power
Success should be handled wisely or enemies are made.

Uruz
"oo-ruse" ᚢ

Aurochs
Life force
Raw primal power
Physical health
The cosmic seed- Adhumla, when Uruz is used a whole universe can spring forth.
The spark that bursts the seedling from its pod.

Thurisaz
"Thor-is-as" ᚦ

Thorn.
Thurses-Giants.
Thurs causes anguish to women, misfortune makes few men cheerful.
Unconscious forces.
Resistance.
Chaos.
Thunder and lightning.
Life and death.
Conflicts.
Power that clears the way.
The strength of the giants.
Aimed might.
Finding peace through the force of battle.

Ansuz
"An-suz" ᚨ

Odins breath, his first gift to humans.
Oss is aged gautr and prince of Asgard and lord of Valhalla.
Communication.
Inspiration.
The voice of the universe.
Language.
Odin.
Expression.
Conceptualisation.
Inner voice.
The power to speak things into reality.

Raido
"Ride-ho" ᚱ

Ride-journey
Riding is said to be the worst thing for horses,
Reginn forged the finest sword.
Wagon.
Turn of the wheel.
Journey of life.
Path to knowledge.
Right action.
Inner compass.
Taking charge.
Movement.
Living in the moment.

Kenaz
"kay-naz" ᚲ

Torch
Ulcer is fatal to children, death makes a corpse pale.
Fire of creation.
The light of knowledge and intelligence.
Illumination of inner self.
Occult secrets.
The burning fire of creativity.
Brightness.

Gebo
"geh-boo" ᚷ

Generosity brings credit and honour which support ones dignity.it furnishes help and sustenance to all broken men who are devoid of aught else.
Gift.
Fair exchange.
Trade.
Generosity.
Compensation.
Hospitality.
Honour.
The gift of love between partners.
Harmony between siblings.

Wunjo
"wun-yo" ᚹ

Who uses it knows no pain, sorrow or anxiety, and he himself has prosperity and bliss.
Joy
Optimism.
Well being.
Love
Contentment.
Fellowship.
Healing emotional pain.
Happiness.

Hagalaz
"hag-all-az" ᚺ

Hail is the cold grain and shower of sleet and sickness of serpents.

Hail.
Radical change.
Disruptions.
Destruction.
Change.
Chaos.
Clearing obstacles through destructive processes.
The inevitability of fate.
Hail lays waste to the land, but from the destruction comes new life.

Nauthiz
"naw-thiz" ᚾ

Constraint gives scant choice, a naked man is chilled by the frost.
Not this.
Need fire.
Necessity.
Forced growth.
Pause.
Strip away.
No pain, no gain.
Doing what must be done.
Hard work.
Self reliance.

To strip away to reveal what's underneath.

Isa
"ee-saa" ᛁ

Ice is called the broad bridge, the blind man must be led.
Ice.
Frozen.
Stillness.
Stasis.
Immobility.
Focus.
Control.
Calm.
Rest before action.

Jera
"yare-awe" ᛃ

Harvest is the hope of men, when gods let, holy king of heaven, the earth give her bright fruits, to the nobles and the needy.
Harvest.
Right timing.
Year.
Fruitful.
Fertility.
Cycles.
Seasons.
You reap what you sew.

Eihwaz
"eye- warz"

The yew is a tree with rough bark,
hard and fast in the earth, supported by its roots,
a guardian of flame and a joy upon an estate.
Yew.
Spiritual axis.
Yggdrasil.
Bridge between worlds.
Lifes mysteries.
Spiritual journey.
Long road to travel.
Balance.
Energy flow.

Perthro
"per- throw"

Peorð is a source of recreation and amusement to the great, where warriors sit blithely together in the beerhall.
Unknown.
What lies between.
Mystery
Norns.
Fate. magic
Female energy.

Algiz.
"All-giz"

Elk
Protection.
Connection to the gods
Defence.
Awareness.
To stand with arms outstretched singing the rune creates a bridge between yourself and the gods.

Algiz is a good rune for amulets.

Sowilo
"so-veal-oh"

Sun is the light of the world, I bow to the divine decree.
Sun.
Bringer of life.
The light that breaks through the shadows.
Wisdom.
Illuminating.
Guidance.
Wholeness.

Tiwaz
"Tee- waz" ↑

Tyr is a one-handed god;
often has the smith to
blow.
Tyr.
Justice.
Balance.
Law.
Courage.
Self sacrifice.
Strength.

Berkano
"Bur-kano" ᛒ

Birch has the greenest
leaves of any shrub;
Loki was fortunate in his
deceit.
Birch.
Birth.
Fertility.
Potential.
Growth.
Beginings.
Secrets.
Concealment.
Sanctuary.

Ehwaz
"Ey-waz" ᛖ

The horse is a joy to
princes in the presence of
warriors.
A steed in the pride of its
hoofs,
when rich men on
horseback bandy words
about it;
and it is ever a source of
comfort to the restless."
Horse.
Movement.
Trust
Loyalty.
Change.
Progression.
Development.
Teamwork.

Mannaz
"ma-naz" ᛗ

Man is an augmentation of
the dust; great is the claw
of the hawk.
Man. Human
consciousness.
Society.
Thought. Inspiration.
Contemplation.
Human interaction.
Ancestors. Descendants.
The Human genetic line

Laguz
"la-goos"

A waterfall is a River which falls from a mountain-side;
but ornaments are of gold.
Water. Flow.
Unstoppable force. Tides.
Stages of life.
Depths of feeling.
Emotion. Inner journey
Journey over water.

Dagaz
"Day-gaaz"

Day, the glorious light of the Creator, is sent by the Lord;
it is beloved of men, a source of hope and happiness to rich and poor,
and of service to all.
Day. Dawn. Awakening.
Illumination.
What rises must fall, and what falls must rise.
Turning of the wheel.

Ingwaz
"Ing-was"

Ing was first seen by men among the East-Danes, until, followed by his chariot,
he departed eastwards over the waves.
So the Heardingas named the hero. Seed
The God Ing
Health. Vitality.
Sexuality.
Personal growth. Potential.

Othala
"Oh-thall-la"

An estate is very dear to every man, if he can enjoy there in his house whatever is right and proper
In constant Prosperity
Breakthrough
Inevitability of time.
Prosperity. Home.
Estate. Ancestry. Property.
Inheritance.

Notes

Kindreds/Group Practice

- Personal Experience and Advice by H. Cronin

Humans are communal so therefore it is natural for us to want to practice our religion in groups. Heathenry is a very individual path but personally, I've found my practice enhanced and completed by being a part of a Kindred. Some people may not be able to get to a local group and this is fine, it's always worth starting your own if you have the time and drive.

In 2015 I started a group in the county of Essex with the intention of bringing local heathens together. I had a vision of a close-knit group like a family sitting around the table, having a drink and laugh together. Fast forward to 2020 (when we could during the pandemic) and beyond, we still meet every month with an average of 20-30 people attending the moots. We're called the Essex and Hertfordshire Heathens.

Whilst I've learned that many other groups are different, as tribes would've been back in the old days, I will share how I started my group with the hope of inspiring other groups to start.

I started simply with a Facebook group, the joys of modern technology! This I advertised on Heathen pages such as Asatru UK and soon local heathens joined. Within a year we became one of the most active groups in the country.

The method? First and foremost, organise a moot in your local pub or a pub close to the majority of members. Even if only 1 or 2 people turn up, this is an amazing start. If nobody turns up then keep trying, don't be disheartened. After this the best course of action was to travel around our counties and visit historical locations. There are various websites you can use to discover local historical locations. Find a local pub or restaurant, meet there have a drink or a dinner together and then move on or vice versa.

This way we could moot close to people, which encourages them to turn up as well as discovering local gems. I was not aware of all the historical locations in and around Essex and Hertfordshire, many in my kindred feel the same way. Locations such as Iron Age forts, Roman locations, medieval castles and ancient battlefields. All locations where there is a certain energy.

A bond formed within the kindred can become very strong, like a family. Whilst none of the following are in the slightest mandatory, eventually we organically had roles for people. Currently we have a Jarl, Gothi, Bannerman and two rune experts. All are elected

Jarl: The organiser and the one who generally makes the phone calls and bookings!

Gothi: The one who prepares and often performs the rituals. We have one who is elected and also someone who fills in when the Gothi isn't present.

Bannerman: We have a banner we carry to our moots and the Bannerman is in charge of storing it, bringing it to moots and maintaining it with the support of the kindred.

Rune experts: We have yet to name the position but these two are generally the ones people go to for a rune reading or spiritual advice.

Again, these positions aren't necessarily needed or a requirement but they help bring structure to a moot so it's not disorganised. These won't come immediately.

Annual camps, trips outside of your counties or just meeting up for fun can also help build the bond within your kindred.

Write down what you do and keep records of what your kindred does so stories can be passed down to new members and the children of the kindred.

Within time you can even discover sacred spaces. Our kindred has 2 spaces, one in Hertfordshire (the witches circle) and one in Essex (a 3000 year old temple). These spaces don't become sacred over night as described in the blōt section, it takes time to build the energy and keep it there. The UK is full of ancient sites with an energy a local kindred can use, just respect these sites.

To conclude the best way to form a Kindred and help it flourish is consistency and hard work, don't let any setbacks put you off, it is definitely worth it in the end. This is my personal method of creating a kindred, there are many other methods and success stories, like with a lot of other things within Heathenry, just do what feels right.

Heathen Families

As Heathenry grows and new people come to the faith, most of them will bring families with them. Asatru UK hosts a number of family friendly moots annually, on our website https://www.asatruuk.org/ there is an amazing article written by our Gareth Hockin about bringing children to moots, we implore you to check it out.

A regular question we get is about children or Christian spouses. When it comes to children, this advice is given; allow them to decide what they want to be. We are not a preaching religion and we do not go out seeking to convert people or our families. The most we can do is talk to our children, tell them stories of the gods, bring them along to moots and let them participate in rituals if they wish. Another way is to practice regular home rituals with them, this is a great way to involve children and make it fun. Do it when they are ready or you risk putting them off. Encourage it without forcing it.

You can also take them out regularly into nature so they appreciate the outdoors. Many children in the modern world are glued to their screens and disconnected to the world around them. No matter where you are in the world, a park, woodland or some other kind of natural beauty is never far away. Take them out there so they can experience the gods, the spirits and the natural world first hand.

A partner or spouse is a different matter. They have their lives and their own practices, feel free to include them in your practice if they are willing and are respectful. You never know, you might make a Heathen of them one day.

Notes

Depression in a Heathen Context

- A personal view by Xan Folmer the creator of Huginns Heathen Hof that many of our members have found useful

I love this community. I love the open tolerance of the broader Pagan umbrella as well as the well-grounded strength and practicality of Heathenry. There is a reason I am a still Heathen. It's far from perfect, but it never claims to be. Part of that strength comes from acknowledging our own shortcomings and working to improve them, both as individuals and as a community. Which is why I chose to write today about something our community doesn't like to talk about.

The Heathen community doesn't deal well with mental illness or depression. There. I said it.

I've written before about how our community puts such a powerful emphasis on the value of self-reliance (not to mention a certain amount of machismo) that asking for help can be a real struggle. As a Heathen I've often felt like talking about depression was more likely to get me judged than to help me. For a group that's normally all about Frith and supporting ones fellows, Heathens can be remarkably unhelpful when it comes to mental or emotional struggles. You're more likely to get a brusque 'Man Up' than a friendly ear or constructive advice.

One's faith-based community should be a balm, not a burden. If we can't turn to Kindred or Clergy for support, then what's the point of either? If we shun those among us who are most in need of our help, how can we hope to build real and lasting organizations? Perhaps even more frustrating is the fact that our Lore DOES address these issues, but that's often overlooked. If you want to see how even the strongest and most devoted Heathen can still struggle with depression, you need look no further than The Allfather himself.

Yes Odin, king of Asgard, glorious lord of battle, and master of poets, wrestles with those same inner demons. Throughout the Lore, Odin regularly struggles with issues that those of us who've had to cope with depression can all recognise. The Allfather is not a happy person by nature. Time and again we see him weighed down by regret, and burdened by the weight of fates he cannot control. As his story progresses, this constant struggle changes him as a person. He becomes more and more cynical, eyeing the world with less hope and more scepticism. The Grímnismál offers us some of the clearest signs of this, in Odin's own words no less.

> Huginn ok Muninn
> fljúga hverjan dag
> Jörmungrund yfir;
> óumk ek of Huginn
> at hann aftr né komit,
> þó sjámk meir um Munin.
>
> Huginn and Muninn
> Fly each day
> over the wide world
> I fear for Huginn
> That he may not return to me
> Yet I fear more for Muninn

What does Odin Allfather fear most? Not death. Not Ragnarök, but the loss of his Munr. The Munr is part of the ancient Norse concept of self, and is the word from which the name Muninn is derived. It is the part of the mind which encompasses ones emotions. While it has no real English corollary, the best translation for this word would probably be 'desire', or 'will'. What the Allfather is expressing here is a fear of losing his passion for life; or more precisely, losing his will to live. The one eyed god bears the weight of extraordinary knowledge and not all knowledge brings joy. We see his words in the Hávamál express this same idea when he says, "There is no worse sickness for the wise than to have nothing left to feel passionate about."

That is what Depression looks like. Or at the very least what it CAN look like. Imagine that your mind is an internal combustion engine, and you only have so much fuel to get you through the day. Each task, or interaction, costs you so much fuel until at the end of the day you run out of gas and go to bed. Your average person can choose to devote their resources as they see fit and ration them out to make sure they last until they can 'refuel'. Now imagine that you can't turn off the engine. Now you have to spend resources to get things done, but in-between tasks your engine is still idling, burning fuel. Even more distressing is the fact that you can't even properly 'refuel'. You can never top off the tank, because your engine never stops.

Everything you want to try to complete must be done through the constant background noise of doubt, regret, worry, and fear. Every molehill might as well be a mountain because you have to carry all of that with you. During the hardest points of depression just mustering the energy required to express emotion can be daunting. How can you possibly spare that kind of energy, when you start the day on half a tank and it takes you twice as much energy to accomplish even essential tasks? It doesn't matter if you are aware of it, if you can rationally tell yourself what's happening. There is no magical 'off switch' that you can hit to fix the problem. No amount of willpower will make it disappear.

So what does the Allfather teach us about coping with these issues? It's sure as Hel not that we need to just 'Man up and get over it'. Odin never lacked for strength of will. Depression isn't a symptom of weakness. When just convincing yourself to get out of bed in the morning is a feat, and every interaction with your peers feels like a trial by fire, but you still have to get up and do it anyway, there is no part of that that is WEAK. No, Odin shows us how to find a different kind of strength.

I've said many times before that Heathenry is, above all else, practical. Odin doesn't find some kind of miraculous magical cure, because there isn't one. Instead he fights a war on two fronts every day, battling both the enemies without and within. So where does he get the strength to confront this?

Kith and Kin

Odin said it himself. Cling to that which you are passionate about. It is always easier to fight for those we love than it is to fight for ourselves. We've all seen it. How often have we all let an insult roll off our back only to find that 'last straw' when we hear our loved ones attacked? Even when it would be such a simple thing to just give up because we don't have the energy to spare on giving a crap, when family calls (blood or otherwise) we find a way. We all have people who rely on us; spouses who deserve a functional partner, children who depend on us for life, parents who gave everything they had so that we could flourish, friends who need to know they can call on us when times are hard, because they would do the same for us.

That's why it is so especially heinous to see these people being berated and belittled by those who should be their source of strength and inspiration. These people mustered up the strength of will to face the world, and then the courage to ask for help from their fellows, only to be called weak by the very thing that should be helping them to carry on. When we see those among our community asking for help, the last thing they need to hear is 'Get over it'. The proper answer is right there in our own tradition.

Notes

Some Important Heathen Dates

Whilst we have no religious dogma or much information about these specific dates, here are some days for your calendar if you don't have a copy of the Asatru UK calendar. The most notable and often most celebrated dates within Heathenry are Midsummer/Summer Solstice, Winter Nights and Yule. Dates, rites and rituals for these dates as well as more information can be found online as it varies greatly. (Each year our annual calendar specifies the dates for that year)

- **Thorsblot/Þorrablót**
- **Dísablót**
- **Hrēþablōt/Sigrblót**
- **Easter/Ēoster**
- **May Day/Þrimilci-daeg**
- **Midsummer/Līþa/Midsommar**
- **Lammas**
- **Winter Nights/Vetrnætr**
- **Yule/Gēola/Jól**
- **Mother's Night/Mōdraniht** – December 24th

Notes

Recommended Reading List

Asatru UK Publications - On Amazon

- **The Travel Hávamál**
- **The Travel Voluspa**
- **The Hávamál: Sayings of the High One**
- **Hávamál: Views and Commentaries**
- **AUK Book of Blóts** (Edited by Dan Coultas)

Affiliated Publications

- **The Gods Own County: A Heathen Prayer Book** by Dan Coultas (Heathens of Yorkshire 2019)

Introductory books

General

- **Ásatrú for Beginners** by Mathias Nordvig (Rockridge Press 2020)
- **The Norse Myths** by Kevin Crossley Holland (Penguin Books 1980)
- **Norse Mythology** by Neil Gaiman (Bloomsbury 2017)

- **A Practical Heathen's Guide to Asatru** by Patricia M. Lafayllve
- **Norse Revival: Transformations of Germanic Neopaganism** by Stefanie von Schnurbein (Brill 2016). https://brill.com/view/title/31763 (Legal and Free)

Primary Sources

- **Edda by Snorri Sturluson,** translated by Anthony Faulkes
- **The Prose Edda** translated by Caroline Larrington

Runes

- **Runes: An Introduction** by R.W.V. Elliot, 2nd Edition (Manchester University Press, 1989)
- **Rune Primer** by Sweyn Plowright (Lulu. Com, 2013)
- **Rudiments of Runelore** by Stephen Pollington (Anglo-Saxon Books 2008)
- **An Introduction to English Runes** by R.I. Page (Boydell Press 2006)
- **Runes and Runic Inscriptions** by Terje Spurklund (Boydell Press 2009)

Fiction

- **Nutcase** by Tony Williams (Salt Publishing, 2017)

(comic book update of Grettis saga, set on a Council Estate)
- **Viking – Odin's Child** (and sequels) by Tim Severin
- **The Way of Wyrd** by Brian Bates (Book Club Associates 1983)
- **Black Shuck 2000 AD** Strip Set in Viking Age

Intermediate

Overview of Mythology

- **Dictionary of Northern Mythology** by Rudolf Simek (D.S. Brewer, New edition 2008)
- **Norse Mythology: A Guide to Gods, Heroes, Rituals, and Beliefs** by John Lindow (Oxford University Press, U.S.A. 2002)
- **The Anglo-Saxon World: An Anthology** Kevin Crossley-Holland (Oxford University Press 2009)
- **Nordic Religion in the Viking Age** by Thomas Dubois (University of Pennsylvania Press 1999)
- **The Viking World** by S Brink and N Price (Routledge 2011)

General "Viking Age" History

- **The Vikings** by Magnus Magnusson (Bodley Head/BBC 1980) – accompanied a TV series, it was also updated by the author

- **Viking - Hammer of the North** by Magnus Magnusson (Orbis 1976)
- **The Hammer and the Cross** by Robert Ferguson (Penguin Books 2010)
- **The Tradition of Household Spirits: Ancestral Lore and Practices** by Claude Lecouteux
- **A Brief History of the Vikings** by Jonathan Clements (Robinson Books 2009)
- **A History of the Vikings** by Gwyn Jones (Book Club Associates 1973)
- **Vikings a History** by Neil Oliver (Weidenfield and Nicolson 2012)

Runes

- **Runes, Magic and Religion: A Sourcebook** by John MacKinnell and Rudolf Simek, with Klaus Düwel (2004)
- **Runic Amulets and Magic Objects** by Mindy MacLeod and Bernard Mees (Boydell Press, 2006)
- **Runes: A Handbook** by Michael P. Barnes (Boydell Press, 2012)

Academic books about Neo-Paganism

- **Nine Worlds of Seid-Magic** by Jenny Blain (Routledge 2002)

- **American Heathens** by Jennifer Snook (Temple University Press 2015)
- **Contemporary Pagan and Native Faith Movements in Europe** by Kathryn Rountree (Berghahn books 2015)

Sagas (there are many editions and translations these are just examples)

- **Edda** by Snorri Sturluson, translated by Anthony Faulkes (Everyman, 1987)
- **The Prose Edda**, transl. by Carolyne Larrington (Oxford University Press, 1996)
- **Beowulf** (many translations available but the one by Seamus Heaney is well regarded)
- **Laxdaela Saga** transl. M. Magnusson & H. Palsson (Penguin Classics 1969)
- **Njal's Saga** transl. M. Magnusson & H. Palsson (Penguin Classics 1960)
- **Grettir's Saga** transl. Jesse Byock (Oxford University Press, 2009)
- **Egil's Saga** transl. H. Palsson (Penguin Books 1967)
- **The Vinland Sagas** transl. M. Magnusson & H. Palsson (Penguin Books 1965)

- **Hrafnkels Saga & other stories** transl. H. Palsson (Penguin Books 1971)
- **Erbyggja Saga** transl. by H Palsson & P Edwards (Penguin Books 1972)
- **Orkneyinga Saga** transl. by H Palsson & P Edwards (Penguin Books 1978)

  All the sagas can be downloaded here for free https://sagadb.org/downloads

Advanced

- **Viking Friendship - The Social Bond in Iceland and Norway, c. 900-1300** By J V Sigurdsson (Cornell University Press 2017)
- **Tracing Old Norse Cosmology** by Anders Andrén (Nordic Academic Press 2014)
- **Myth and Religion of the North: The Religion of Ancient Scandinavia** by E.O.G. Turville-Petre (Weidenfeld and Nicolson, 1964)
- **Gods and Myths of Northern Europe** by H.R. Ellis Davidson (Penguin, 1964)
- **Scandinavian Mythology by** H.R. Ellis Davidson (Paul Hamlyn, 1969)

- **Iron Age Myth and Materiality: An Archaeology of Scandinavia AD 400-1000** by Lotte Hedeager (Routledge 2011)
- **Myths and Symbols in Pagan Europe: Early Scandinavian and Celtic Religions** by H.R. Ellis Davidson (Manchester University Press, 1988)
- **The Lost Beliefs of Northern Europe** by H.R. Ellis Davidson (Routledge, 1993)
- **The Lost Gods of England** by Brian Branston (Book Club 1974)
- **Myths of the Pagan North: The Gods of the Norsemen by Christopher Abram** (Hambledon Continuum, 2011)
- **Old Norse Religion in Long-term Perspectives: Origins, Changes and Interactions** by Anders Andrén (Nordic Academic Press 2006)
- **- Viking Worlds: Things Spaces and Movement** by Marianne Hem Erikson (Oxbow Books 2019)
- **- Sacred to the Touch: Nordic and Baltic Religious Wood Carving** by Thomas A. DuBois (University of Washington Press 2017)

Seiðr & Magic

- **Texts & Contexts of the Oldest Runic Inscription** by Tineke J.H. Looijenga (Brill 2003)

- **Witchcraft and Magic in the Nordic Middle Ages** by Stephen A. Mitchell (University of Pennsylvania Press 2013)
- **Shamanism in Norse Myth and Magic** - Clive Tolley (Finnish Academy of Science & Letters, 2009)
- **Magic Staffs in the Viking Age** by Leszek Gardela (Forlag Fassbaender 2016)
- **The Viking Way** by Neil S. Price (Oxbow Books 2009)

Childrens books

- **D'Aulaires Book of Norse Myths** by Ingri and Edgar D'Aulaire (NYRB Children's Collection 2006)
- **D'Aulaires Book of Trolls** by Ingri and Edgar D'Aulaire (NYRB Children's Collection 2006)
- **The Riddle of the Runes** by Janina Ramirez (OUP Oxford 2018)
- **Make this Viking Settlement** by Iain Ashman (Usborne Publishing Ltd 2009)
- **Viking Raiders** by Anne Civardi (Usborne Publishing Ltd 1998)
- **The Saga of Erik the Viking** by Terry Jones and Michael Foreman (Puffin 1988)

- **Norse Myths and Legends** by Cheryl Evans, Anne Millard and Rodney Matthews (Usborne Publishing Ltd 2006)
- **Odd and the Frost Giants** by Neil Gaiman and Mark Buckingham (Bloomsbury Publishing PLC 2010)
- **Trolls and Their Relatives** by Jan Bergh Eriksen and Per Aase (Dreyer Bok 1988)

Other Resources

Audiobooks

- **Norse Mythology - Neil Gaiman** – Unabridged ISBN 0062663631, ISBN 1489452443 ISBN 0062834487
- **Norse Mythology** - Neil Gaiman – BBC dramatized version, ISBN 1787534618
- **Children of Odin** - Padraic Colum (Mp3 CD) ISBN 1775424340
- **Poems of the Elder Edda** - Patricia Terry ISBN 139781940650043, Audible and iTunes
- **Poetic Edda** - Jackson Crawford ISBN 198259750X
- **Saga of the Volsungs & Ragnar Lothbrok** - Jackson Crawford, ISBN 1982604689

- **The Great Courses: Vikings** – a series of lectures by Kenneth W. Harl, and aimed at a broad audience (Audible)

Books on related topics

- **Westward to Vinland** - the discovery of the Norse settlement in Newfoundland by Helge Ingstad (Jonathan Cape 1969)
- **Scandinavian Legends and Folktales retold** by Gwyn Jones original publication 1956 (Oxford University Press 1995)

Adult fiction set in the Viking Age

- **The Whale Road** (and sequels) by Robert Low
- **The Last Kingdom** (and sequels) by Bernard Cornwell
- **Blood Feud** by Rosemary Sutcliffe (Quercus 2018)
- **God of Vengeance** (and sequels) by Giles Kristian
- **Eaters of the Dead** by Michael Crichton (Arrow 1997)
- **The Burning Black: Legend of Black Shuck** - Graphic Novel set in Elizabethan England
- **Days in Midgard: A Thousand Years On** by Steven T. Abell (Outskirts Press 2008)

Others

- **Last Places** by Lawrence Millman (Andre Deutsch 1990)

Online Resources

The Road to Hel by H.R. Ellis - A Study of the Conception of the Dead in Old Norse Literature

http://www.germanicmythology.com/scholarship/road_to_hel.pdf

Viking Society for Northern Research (VSNR)

http://vsnrweb-publications.org.uk/

The Icelandic Saga Database

http://sagadb.org/

Icelandic Saga Map

http://sagamap.hi.is/is/

Mimisbrunnr: Developments in Ancient Germanic Studies

https://www.mimisbrunnr.info/

Futhark: International Journal of Runic Studies

http://futhark-journal.com/

The Pomegranate: the International journal of Pagan studies

https://journals.equinoxpub.com/index.php/POM

Dr Jackson Crawford

https://www.youtube.com/c/JacksonCrawford/

Dr Mathias Nordvig

https://www.youtube.com/user/mattndk

https://nordicmythologychannel.com/

Dr Rune Rasmussen

https://www.youtube.com/user/Runehr/

https://www.nordicanimism.com/

Dr Alaric Hall

https://www.alarichall.org.uk/resources.php

Scandia: Journal of Medieval Norse Studies

https://periodicos.ufpb.br/index.php/scandia/issue/archive

RMN Newsletter (Retrospective Methods Network)

https://www.helsinki.fi/en/networks/retrospective-methods-network/archive

Academia.edu

https://www.academia.edu/

Notes

Notes